Jesus
Heals a Man

Bibleworld Books contains stories adapted
from the *Contemporary English Version* of the Bible.
Each book is designed to provide early readers with a text
adapted from Scripture in a form and manner that helps them
develop their reading skills and introduce them to the narrative of the Bible.

Adapted from:
Mission Literacy Readers Level 1 & 2
© 2008 American Bible Society
Used by permission.

Jesus Heals a Man is based on Mark 2:1-12

ISBN: 978-0-901518-73-6

Series 1: Book 2

Illustrated by Graeme Hewitson

© 2017 The Scottish Bible Society (Formerly The National Bible Society of Scotland).
Company number SC238687, Scottish Charity SC010767
All rights reserved.

The Scottish Bible Society
7 Hampton Terrace, Edinburgh. EH12 5XU
www.scottishbiblesociety.org

Series 1: Who was Jesus

Jesus and the Storm
Jesus Heals a Man
Jesus Feeds a Crowd
Jesus Walks on the Water

Bibleworld Books provides three full session outlines to accompany each story book with games and activities designed to raise each child's learning potential.

Available for free download at www.bibleworld.co.uk

These men were friends.

They had another friend, who could not walk.

When somebody told them that Jesus healed people they said,

"Maybe he will help our friend!"

They went and picked up their friend...

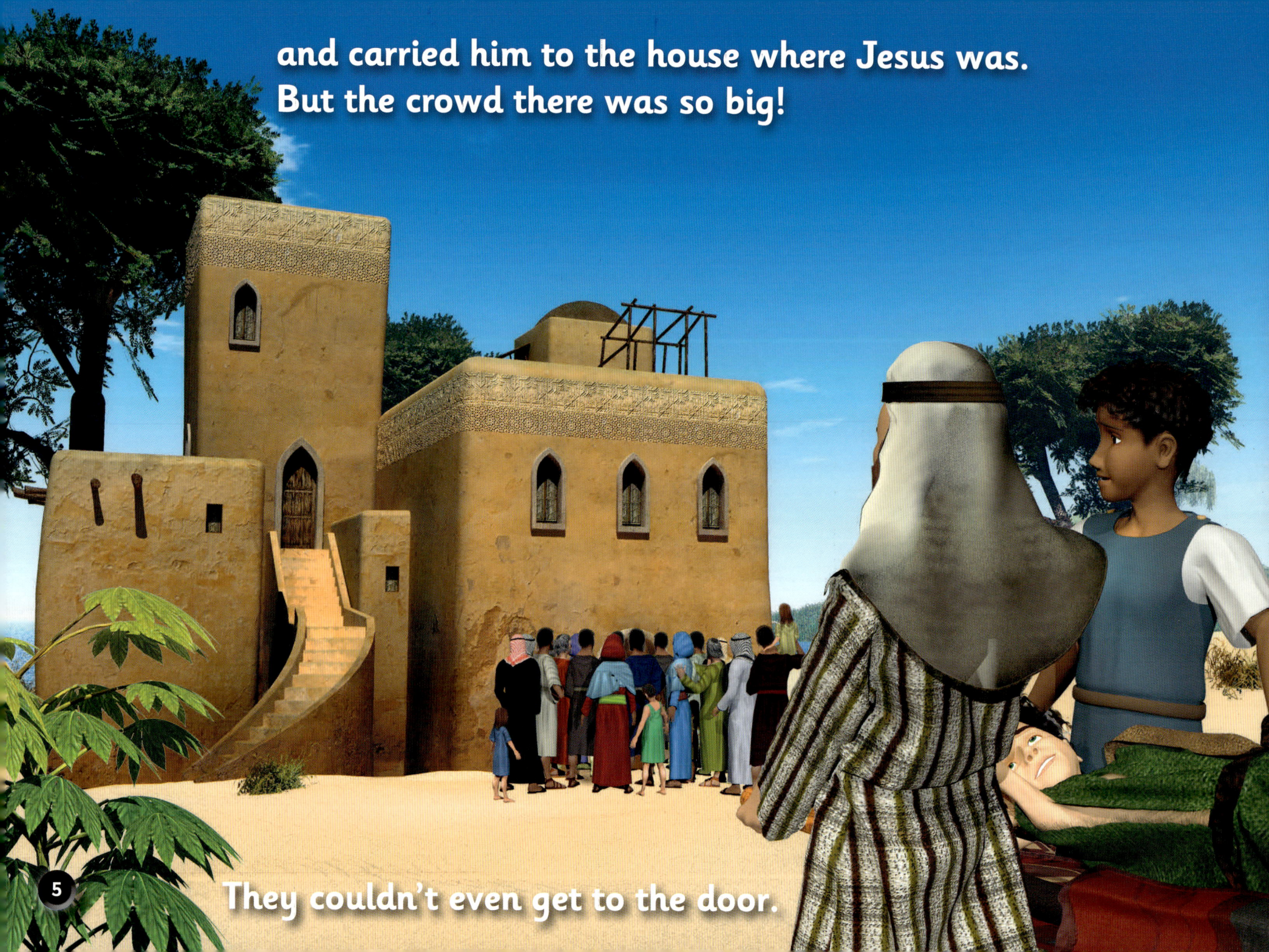
and carried him to the house where Jesus was. But the crowd there was so big!

They couldn't even get to the door.

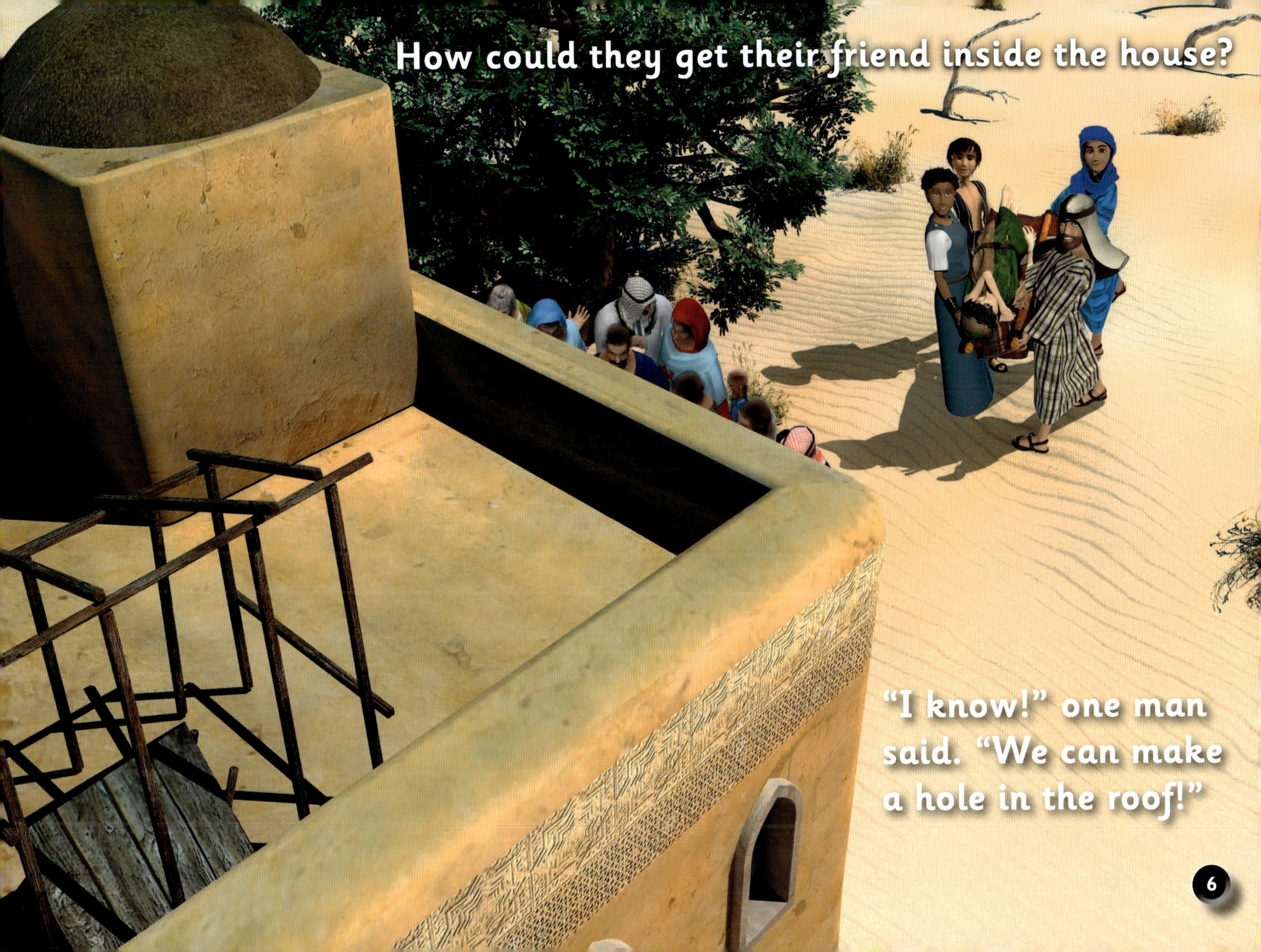

How could they get their friend inside the house?

"I know!" one man said. "We can make a hole in the roof!"

They took their friend up on the roof, and put ropes underneath him.

Then they made a hole in the roof and lowered him down into the house.

They wanted him to be close to Jesus.

Some teachers who were there didn't like that at all.

"Who does he think he *is?*" they wondered.

Jesus knew what they were thinking.

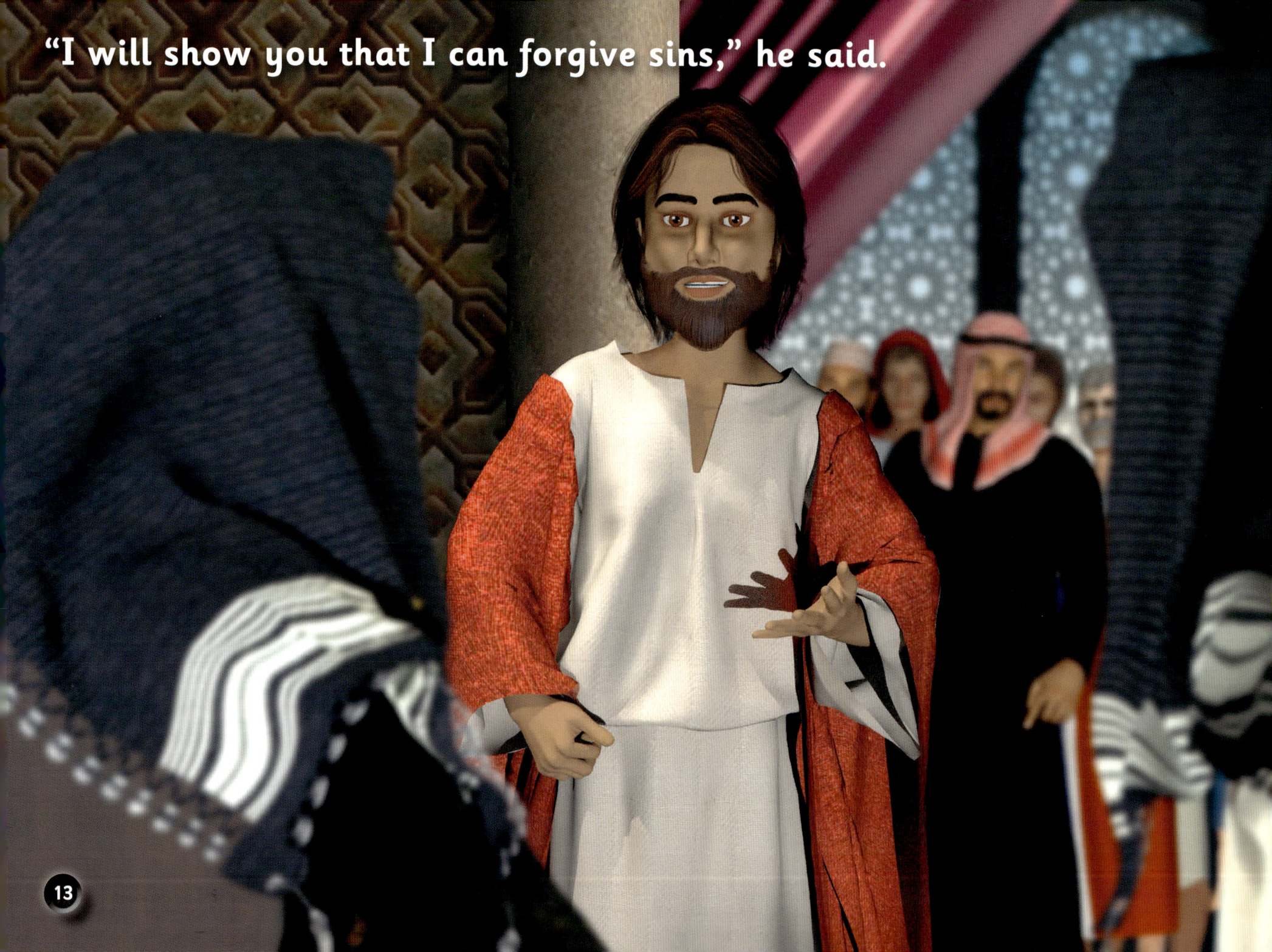
"I will show you that I can forgive sins," he said.

The man got right up! He picked up his mat...

and he walked out the door!